THE WISDOM
OF THANKFULNESS

Researched, compiled, and written by

Toni Armstrong Sample

THE WISDOM
OF THANKFULNESS

Researched, compiled, and written by

Toni Armstrong Sample

Based on a conversation with
Peg Sample about the blessing of a thankful heart,
further inspiration from God's Word,
and individual stories of thankfulness.

INDEX

Forward

A Little about Toni

Tomorrow
Fullness
Encouragement
Growth
Relationships
Perseverance
Enlightenment
Peace and Contentment

Forward

Many people with wise hearts and wise minds have experienced
the wisdom of thankfulness.
They have infused and enriched our lives through what
they have learned,
and, through their words, they have shown their
desire to pass on to us those lessons of life.

Rather than reinvent the wheel – I pass on to you the
wisdom of others and the wisdom of God,
adding my thoughts and comments.

The words of wisdom of thankfulness of others
have touched my heart.

It is my desire and the desire of Peg, who discussed the
initial idea of this book with me, that the contents
of this book, the values found within,
will be of significant influence
to you and future generations. I dedicate this
book to Peg and our families.

With much love,
Toni Armstrong Sample

A Little about Toni

Toni Armstrong Sample, retired Human Resource Management Executive, is currently an author, artist, and speaker.

Growing up in the small town of Centerville, Pennsylvania, and beginning her education in a one-room schoolhouse, seems almost surreal in today's world. She was born into a family that had its kinks and bruises. Today it would be called dysfunctional. Toni believes that her family was functional, like the majority of rural families in those days. Toni, raised in a family of flawed parents with less than perfect children, had a childhood that reflected the morality of her loving and caring God.

Toni has been bruised and battered along life's way. You may want to read her autobiographical books – "I'll Never Be the Same," "A Buck Three Eighty," and "I Got Here as Fast as I Could."

Like most everyone, Toni has lost people she loved very much. She also was furloughed from a job because it was 'eliminated,' was betrayed by people she trusted, moved from town-to-town and state-to-state, and learned to say hello and goodbye many more times than she ever wanted.

If I were to use one word to describe my life – that word would be 'impermanent.' And, yet, for what little is permanent and the abundance of what is current, I am grateful and content.

Toni desires the readers of "The Wisdom of Thankfulness" to enjoy these quotes and the stories that go with them. After hearing of Peg's desire that her family and others would be grateful for their blessings, she was motivated to write this book. It is a blessing to become aware of the joy one receives from the simple act of thanks. I join Peg in her belief that the topic of appreciation is an essential part of our lives.

Hearts that are rich with gratitude are abounding with love. Do grateful hearts beat more robust, longer, or steadier because of the recognition of our blessings? Probably not. But, every beat of our hearts – 117,120 beats a day – has meaning.

TOMORROW

**"Gratitude makes sense of our past,
brings peace for today,
and creates a vision for tomorrow."**
Melody Beattie

Melody Beattie is an American author of self-help books on codependent relationships.

Beattie graduated from high school with honors. Melody began drinking at age 12, was a full-blown alcoholic by age 13, and was a junkie by age 18.

Beattie authored 18 books, including:
Codependent No More, Beyond Codependency
The Language of Letting Go
Make Miracles in Forty Days: Turning What You Have into What You Want, published in 2010.

Several of her books are so beneficial that they are available in languages other than English.

***

Thoughts from Toni:

Isn't it interesting that a person who has faced so many battles could be thankful?

Melody, in her biographical introduction, doesn't tell her readers that along with her addiction battles, she lost a son, in 1991, to a skiing accident.

Despite all the pain and disillusionment of her life -- still, she is thankful.

What is the foundation of a grateful heart?   Those who read about Melody's life are impressed that she can look through the foggy mirror of her years and see a past that makes sense. She is not blaming anyone for what has happened to her. How did she achieve the maturity that shows itself as a heart full of appreciation and compassion?

Melody has made peace with her past and looks forward to her future. She is resilient and pliable in a rigid world, not giving way to what was but standing tall and strong in preparation for what might be.

***

What does God tell us about this kind of gratefulness?

Joshua 1:9 ESV

***Have I not commanded you? Be strong and courageous.
Do not be frightened, and do not be dismayed, for
the Lord your God is with you wherever you go."***

2 Timothy 1:7 ESV

For God gave us a spirit not of fear but of power and love and self-control.

Isaiah 41:10 ESV

Fear not, for I am with you; be not dismayed, for I am your God; I will strengthen you, I will help you, I will uphold you with my righteous right hand.

Philippians 4:13 ESV

I can do all things through him who strengthens me.

Ephesians 6:10 ESV

Finally, be strong in the Lord and in the strength of his might.

***

Our prayer is that as our hearts grow with gratefulness, so will our peace, our vision for tomorrow, and our ability to withstand whatever this life presents. It is with hearts overflowing with love that we put yesterday behind us and not looking back turn toward the promise of tomorrow.

Bible Study Questions

Tomorrow

Like Melody, have you ever experienced deep hurt and disillusionment in your life and were still able to maintain a posture of thankfulness and compassion?

Be honest as you answer this question. To you, what is the foundation of a grateful heart?

Looking back, are you able to see God at work in your life?

Melody has experienced drug addiction, the loss of her son, and other tragedies of life, has made peace with her past, and looks forward to her future. Do you understand that kind of resilience and how God's mercy has endowed her with peace and hope for tomorrow?

FULLNESS:

**"Gratitude unlocks the fullness of life.
It turns what we have into enough and more.
It turns denial into acceptance,
chaos to order,
confusion to clarity.
It can turn a meal into a feast,
a house into a home,
a stranger into a friend."**
Melody Beattie

***

Thoughts from Toni:

You already know a bit about Melody's background. We can appreciate her transparency and desire to share with others how she understands and appreciates that gratitude enriches her life. Together, let's think about her words.

Gratitude – our appreciation for our minds and bodies, our families and friends, and our achievements and failures, is enough. Enough? By thinking 'enough,' we believe we do not need or want more.

Dissecting Melody's quote, she appreciates the fortunate circumstance of living the American dream without being greedy. Being grateful, we find joy in living that dream. The recognition of who provides our blessings produces a humble and indebted way to look at life.

Another factor evident in Melody's life is not denying her faults and shortcomings but accepting them as part of who she is. As she speaks of her flaws and the mountains she has climbed, Melody identifies her imperfections as the Creator's way of making her unique and wonderful.

She is grateful that He has strengthened her through the difficulties she experienced. Melody suggests that when life is full of confusion and disorder, which it often can be, being thankful even for those difficult times can turn horror into joy. If every day went exactly as we planned and desired, how could, or would, we appreciate a better time?

As the saying goes, "There are two sides to every coin."

Gratitude unlocks the door that allows someone we have never known to become a friend.

God constructed the human heart, our soul, our spirit, to be filled by the fullness of relationship.

As difficult as it is to dig into a hardened -- unloving, uncaring, ungrateful heart -- it is that tough exterior that cries out for friendship.

Who cares enough to approach, listen, appreciate, and be grateful for a stranger who may become a friend?

***

What does God tell us about relationships?

1 Thessalonians 5:11 ESV

Therefore encourage one another and build one another up, just as you are doing.

Proverbs 4:23 ESV

Keep your heart with all vigilance, for from it flow the springs of life.

Proverbs 17:17 ESV

A friend loves at all times, and a brother is born for adversity.

Ephesians 4:2-3 ESV

With all humility and gentleness, with patience, bearing with one another in love, eager to maintain the unity of the Spirit in the bond of peace.

***

Our prayer is that you will find a gentleness in your soul that permits you to look at the acts of others and forgive what may be hurtful. Look at your brothers and sisters, your neighbors all over the earth, and see that God created everyone to do good and have good relationships. Show everyone love and the opportunity to learn how relationships and forgiveness can bring joy and peace.

Bible Study Questions

Fullness

Melody Beattie, in this study, has moved beyond her past to a brighter tomorrow.   In this lesson, we move on to Fullness.

Do you agree with Melody that gratitude is what unlocks the fullness of life?   If not, what does?

Have you ever tried to deny something you don't want to admit? If so, has gratitude to God for the fullness of your life helped you to accept those things you want to deny?

Melody tells us that gratitude creates clarity and order in our life? Explain what you think she means.

Can gratitude turn a house into a home, a meal into a feast, a stranger into a friend?   How?

ENCOURAGEMENT

**At times our own light goes out
and is rekindled by a spark
from another person.
Each of us has cause to think
with deep gratitude
of those who have
lighted the flame within us.**
Albert Schweitzer

Albert Schweitzer was a Theologian, Philosopher, Journalist, Scholar, Missionary, Doctor, and Preacher (1875-1965)

He was born in the German province of Alsace-Lorraine.

He wrote "The Quest of the Historical Jesus," was a music scholar and organist, and a mission doctor in Gabon, Africa.

He was awarded the Nobel Peace Prize in 1952, with his "The Problem of Peace" lecture considered one of the best.

From 1952 until his death, he worked against nuclear tests and weapons with Albert Einstein, Otto Hahn, and Bertrand Russell.

***

Thoughts from Toni:

With all the drive and success that this amazing man of our times had, isn't it interesting that he speaks about the deep gratitude he held for those who reignited his direction and focus in his quote above?

It is our obligation to our fellow man to be encouragers. When life gets us down, we want someone to lend us a hand, say a kind word, smile at us, reinforce that we are worthwhile. The great Albert Schweitzer understood that in all his greatness, he was still just a human -- with all the frailness and weakness that comes with being human. His gratitude to others shows his greatness.

This quote reminds us of the poem by John Donne, "No Man Is an Island." Sometimes we forget that we are not 'stand-alone' beings. We are all interconnected, and through this connection, we help each other.

No Man is an Island
by John Donne

No man is an island, Entire of itself,
Every man is a piece of the continent,
A part of the main.
If a clod be washed away by the sea,
Europe is the less.
As well as if a promontory were.
As well as if a manor of thy friend's
Or of thine own were:
Any man's death diminishes me,
Because I am involved in mankind,
And therefore send not to know for whom the bell tolls;
It tolls for thee

***

What does God tell us about encouragement?

Jeremiah 29:11 ESV

For I know the plans I have for you, declares the LORD, plans for welfare and not for evil, to give you a future and a hope.

1 Thessalonians 5:11 ESV

Therefore encourage one another and build one another up, just as you are doing.

Isaiah 41:10 ESV

Fear not, for I am with you; be not dismayed, for I am your God; I will strengthen you, I will help you, I will uphold you with my righteous right hand.

Ephesians 4:29 ESV

Let no corrupting talk come out of your mouths, but only such as is good for building up, as fits the occasion, that it may give grace to those who hear.

Hebrews 10:25(a) ESV

Not neglecting to meet together, as is the habit of some, but encouraging one another...

Romans 15:4 ESV

For whatever was written in former days was written for our instruction, that through endurance and through the encouragement of the Scriptures we might have hope.

Proverbs 3:5-6 ESV

Trust in the LORD with all your heart, and do not lean on your own understanding. In all your ways acknowledge him, and he will make straight your paths.

***

Our prayer is that you will always be uplifted and encouraged to continue this walk of life that can, at times, be extremely difficult. We were created, not to be alone, but to live in partnership with another. Take kind and polite counsel from others who offer you the love and caring of their hearts. Whenever possible, encourage those around you, for everyone needs to feel of value and be uplifted.

Bible Study Questions

Encouragement

You may not have been aware of all the positions and accomplishments of Albert Schweitzer, but you are probably aware of the outstanding contributions he made to humankind.

In his opening quote, were you surprised that Albert Schweitzer would admit that at times 'his light would go out' and that he would need a spark from another person to rekindle his focus?

Have you ever been in a similar position, needing someone to encourage you in an endeavor?

Can you name an endeavor you have taken on in which you lost interest or focus, and someone helped you get back on track?

Were you grateful to that person, and did you show your gratitude?

GROWTH

**Be true to yourself, help others,
make each day your masterpiece,
make friendship a fine art,
drink deeply from good books
- especially the Bible,
build a shelter against a rainy day,
give thanks for your blessings
and pray for guidance every day.
John Wooden**

John Robert Wooden (1910-2010), nicknamed the "Wizard of Westwood," was an American basketball player and head coach at UCLA. In his coach position, his teams won ten NCAA national championships in 12 years and the men's basketball-record of winning 88 consecutive games. His teams also won seven consecutive NCAA Championships - no other coach or school has won more than two straight years.

Wooden was named the national coach of the year six times and was highly valued and respected by his players, including Kareem Abdul-Jabbar.

Wooden was renowned for his short, simple inspirational messages to his players, including his "Pyramid of Success." These often were directed at how to be a success in life as well as in basketball.

Readers of Coach **Wooden's Pyramid of Success** received practical, down to earth, biblical tips for being successful in life. Readings based on **Wooden's** own life experiences and spiritual development through the years revealed that **success** is built block by block, much like a **pyramid**.

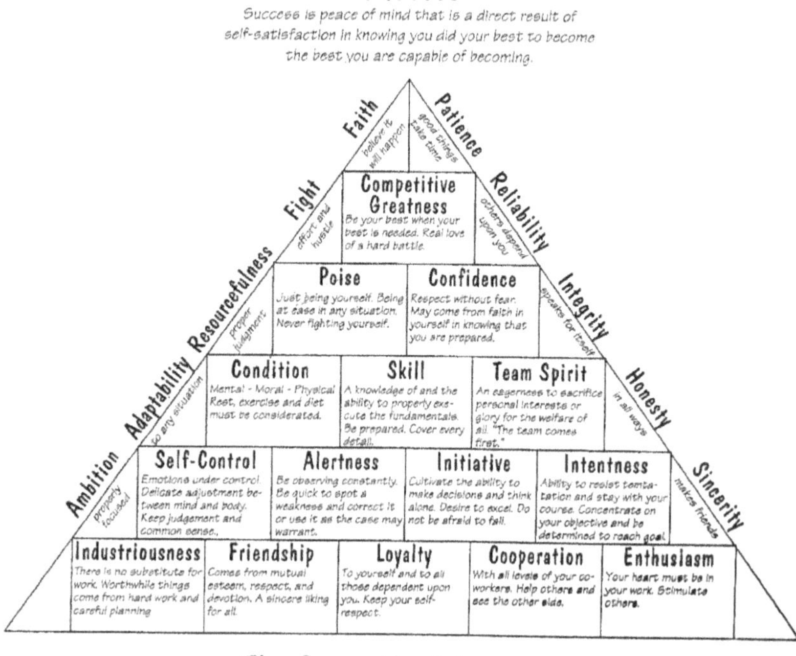

***

Thoughts from Toni:

John Wooden believed in helping his players grow in their values. How comfortable are his words to put into practice? It would be easier to make a basket from the free-throw line than to achieve all these pieces of wisdom.

Be true to yourself. What does that mean? Don't lie, cheat, steal, or behave in such a way that you would not be proud of you. Be true to the person you are worthy of being.

Help others. How often do we put off helping someone and miss the opportunity? Helping someone means providing what they need when they need it—not doing what you want to do when you have spare time or feel like it.

Make each day your masterpiece. Do your best to be your best – every day.

Make friendship a fine art. One of my favorite quotes is Martin Lutheran King's. "In the end, we will remember not the words of our enemies but the silence of our friends." I used to think of my friends' silence – then I thought about my friends and my silence.

Drink deeply from good books – especially the Bible. Let the excellent and faithful words of others help to direct your path. But, like false prophets – be careful of the words you follow. Do some research and make sure they are the right words that will lead you to peace and a life of contentment and fullness.

Build a shelter against a rainy day. Preparing for the unexpected means build a savings account, bodily strength and health, and spiritual muscle.

Give thanks for your blessings, and pray for guidance every day. Be grateful for life and the guiding force that walks with us. Start each day with a prayer. If that is foreign to you – try this one: "Dear God, Thank you for this day. Help me as I move through these 24 hours. Keep me safe and in your care. Be with those I love, and even those who don't love me. Amen

***

What does God tell us about growth?

<u>Philippians 1:6</u> ESV

And I am sure of this, that he who began a good work in you will bring it to completion.

<u>Philippians 4:13</u> ESV

I can do all things through him who strengthens me.

<u>Galatians 5:22-23</u> ESV

The fruit of the Spirit is love, joy, peace, patience, kindness, goodness, faithfulness, gentleness, self-control.

<u>1 Corinthians 13:10</u>ESV

When I was a child, I spoke like a child, I thought like a child, I reasoned like a child. When I became a man, I gave up childish ways.

<u>1 Peter 2:1</u>ESV

So put away all malice and all deceit and hypocrisy and envy and all slander.

<u>James 1:2</u> ESV

And let steadfastness have its full effect, that you may be perfect and complete, lacking in nothing.

<u>Matthew 19:26</u> (b) ESV

"With man this is impossible, but with God all things are possible."

Isaiah 40:31 ESV

They shall mount up with wings like eagles; they shall run and not be weary; they shall walk and not faint.

2 Peter 1:6 ESV

And knowledge with self-control, and self-control with steadfastness, and steadfastness with godliness,

Hebrews 12:14 (a) ESV

Strive for peace with everyone

2 Timothy 1:7 ESV

For God gave us a spirit not of fear but of power and love and self-control.

***

Our prayer is one of thanking God for allowing us to grow in his grace and mercy; that we might put away those parts of the spirit that are not pleasing to God.   And that we might rise on wings like eagles, filled with love, peace, patience, gentleness, kindness, self-control, and steadfast devotion to our Creator.

Bible Study Questions

Growth

Reading John Wooden's opening quote, do you believe you are true to yourself? If so, how?   If not, why?

Are you filling each day with things that are worthwhile, meaningful, and helpful to others?

How do you establish and maintain valuable friendships? Or, do you leave it to your friends to do the hard work?

Do you spend time each day reading from the Bible and other books of quality?

Do you give thanks for your blessings and ask God to guide you through each day?

Are you building a shelter for a rainy day? If you are, describe your shelter.

RELATIONSHIPS

**None of us got to where we are alone.
Whether the assistance we received
was obvious or subtle,
acknowledging someone's help
is a big part of understanding
the importance of saying thank you.**

Harvey Mackay

Harvey Mackay (born 1932) is a businessman, author, and syndicated columnist.

His weekly column gives career and inspirational advice, featured in over 100 newspapers.

Mackay has authored seven *New York Times* bestselling books, including three number one bestsellers.

In 1988, Mackay wrote his first book, *Swim with the Sharks without Being Eaten Alive.*

He is a member of the National Speakers Association Council of Peers Award for Excellence Hall of Fame.

He is married, has three children and eleven grandchildren, is an outstanding volunteer, serves on many Boards, is an entrepreneur, and received recognition with many awards.

***

Thoughts from Toni:

The first thing that strikes me as I read the short biography of Harvey Mackay and his quote at the beginning of this chapter is, "how interesting that such a highly regarded and successful man appreciates those that helped him along the way."

Deeply involved, intelligent, and busy people occasionally get pulled down by their ego. They can forget how they reached the pinnacle of their achievements.

Harvey understands that sometimes help comes as an apparent force, and, at other times, it comes from behind the scenes – barely noticed, unless you pause to reflect on how the door opened that we walked through. And, going one step further, understanding the importance of acknowledgment and saying, "Thank you."

If you've ever watched how Hollywood, Broadway, or Nashville acknowledges their great successes – each awardee is encouraged to 'thank' those who helped them achieve their recognition.

When I listen to these award shows and others, I often hear humility as people thank, first the other competitors.

How many of us, in ordinary life, ever think to thank those who come along beside us, urging us to do better and better and be all that we can be? That's what competitors do. They give us a scale by which to measure our strength and endurance for the race.

Award recipients then thank their parents, spouses, children, and family members who supported and encouraged them along the way.

Next will be all those on the 'team.' Yes, 'the team' – we all have one. Maybe not a legal team, but everyone who works together to accomplish something is our team.

We have teams in our work, our churches, our communities, many of our hobbies, and even our volunteer work. The most crucial team that many belong to is our family and friends, who support and encourage us to greater heights. We don't accomplish much alone – it takes a 'village.'

***

What does God say to us about team relationships?

<u>Proverbs 27:17</u> ESV

Iron sharpens iron, and one man sharpens another.

<u>1 Corinthians 12:20</u> ESV

There are many parts, yet one body. The eye cannot say to the hand, "I have no need of you," nor again the head to the feet, "I have no need of you."

<u>1 Peter 4:10</u> ESV

As each has received a gift, use it to serve one another, as good stewards of God's varied grace

<u>Hebrews 10:24-25</u> ESV

Stir up one another to love and good works, not neglecting to meet together, as is the habit of some, but encouraging one another.

Ephesians 4:32 ESV

Be kind to one another, tenderhearted, forgiving

Philippians 2:3-4 ESV

Do nothing from rivalry or conceit, but in humility count others more significant than yourselves. Let each of you look not only to his own interests, but also to the interests of others.

Galatians 6:2 ESV

Bear one another's burdens

Philippians 2:2 ESV

Complete my joy by being of the same mind, having the same love, being in full accord.

Ecclesiastes 4:9 ESV

Two are better than one, because they have a good reward for their toil.

***

Our prayer is to love the Lord our God with all of our hearts and our neighbors as ourselves, to obey the will of God, and to put the needs of others before our own.

Bible Study Questions

Relationships

Who has helped you accomplish the success you have had in any part of your life?

Was this person(s) obvious in their mentorship, or were they helping you from the sidelines, or were they carrying out their position requirements in an exemplary manner – i.e., .teacher, co-worker, supervisor, pastor, etc.?

Have you sought out this person(s), letting them know of the positive influence they had in enriching your life?

PERSEVERANCE

**Whatever we are waiting for
- peace of mind,
contentment, grace,
the inner awareness of simple abundance
– it will surely come to us,
but only when we are ready
to receive it with an open and grateful heart.**

Sarah Ban Breathnach

Sarah became a millionairess with her book, *Simple Abundance*.

In 2009, she fled England, leaving behind her cherished home — once Sir Isaac Newton's chapel — along with her freeloading British husband, and creditors baying for payment.

Since childhood, Sarah's actions have been ruled by her obsessive need to please others

Now living in a tiny rental, her inspiring new book, *Peace and Plenty*, recaptures her gentle voice of gratitude and grit.

***

Thoughts from Toni:

Life can be tricky, even for the ones that make it look easy. Much depends on how we view and face our difficulties. We have choices -- to move forward with resolve, make corrections to our path, and persevere – or we can let our challenges define us.

Sarah was ashamed, she had made bad decisions, and creditors were picking at her bones. She had risen to the mountaintop – and it had overcome her. There was no instant fix. Armed with a ladder of resolve, she forged slowly ahead.

Her words "finding the inner awareness of simple abundance," helps us understand that we, through grace, have been given everything we need for a life of peace and contentment.

Taking it a bit further – she suggests how we can receive this great gift.

Sarah suggests that we search within ourselves, opening our hearts to find and recognize our inherent pool of gratitude. It is then that serenity and satisfaction with ourselves, others, and our life will follow.

***

What does God tell us about perseverance?

Galatians 6:9 ESV

And let us not grow weary of doing good, for in due season we will reap, if we do not give up.

2 Thessalonians 3:13 ESV

As for you, brothers, do not grow weary in doing good.

Romans 5:4 ESV / 662 helpful votes Helpful Not Helpful

And endurance produces character, and character produces hope,

James 5:11 ESV

Behold, we consider those blessed who remained steadfast. You have heard of the steadfastness of Job, and you have seen the purpose of the Lord, how the Lord is compassionate and merciful.

Proverbs 3:5-6 ESV

Trust in the LORD with all your heart, and do not lean on your own understanding. In all your ways acknowledge him, and he will make straight your paths.

1 Corinthians 16:13 ESV

Be watchful, stand firm in the faith, act like men, be strong.

1 Peter 5:7 ESV

Casting all your anxieties on him, because he cares for you.

James 1:4 ESV

And let steadfastness have its full effect, that you may be perfect and complete, lacking in nothing.

***

Our prayer is that we will remain strong in our convictions, filled with hope for the future set before us. We ask for confidence in the knowledge that God has designed the path for those who believe in His Son, Jesus Christ, and follow His Word. The greatest commandment of all is to Love God, Love One Another, and Love Yourself. May God live forever in our hearts and direct our steps.

Bible Study Questions

Perseverance

Like Sarah, are your actions based on a need to please others?

Who is the one person we need to please?

Will pleasing our Savior bring us peace of mind and contentment?

Are you aware of the abundance in your life because you have a God who loves you?   Is your heart filled with gratitude to God for your abundant life?

ENLIGHTENMENT

**When you arise in the morning,
give thanks for the light,
for your life,
for your strength.
Give thanks for your food
and for the joy of living.
If you see no reason to give thanks,
the fault lies in yourself.**

Gabby Douglas

Gabrielle "Gabby" Douglas[1] (born 1995) is the first African American gold medal winner in the individual all-around and team competitions, which occurred during the 2012 Summer Olympics. Gabby was a member of the U.S. Women's Gymnastics team.

One of four children, Gabby, began gymnastics training when she was three. She won her first state championship at age 8.

"I believe in God. He is the secret of my success. He gives people talent, and ... I love sharing about my faith. God has given me this amazing God-given talent, so I'm going to go out and glorify His name."

***

Thoughts from Toni:

Gabby is undoubtedly a role model and inspiration to anyone who aspires to achieve a particular goal.

Her advice is real and humble.

Gabby begins her day with thanks – and continues that thankfulness throughout the day for all that she receives. How many of us start from the rising sun thanking God for all He supplies. Gabby recognizes the Creator's abundant grace as he allows daylight, breath, strength, food, and joy to fill our lives.

Like most Olympians, athletes, competitors, she ends this quote with a delightful dare – "I dare you not to have anything for which to be grateful – and, if you can't, you need to look again."

It is evident that her love for the Lord drives her and that she looks to the finish line, do you?

***

What does God tell us about enlightenment?

Daniel 5:14 ESV

I have heard of you that the spirit of the gods is in you, and that light and understanding and excellent wisdom are found in you.

Ephesians 1:18 ESV

Having the eyes of your hearts enlightened, that you may know what is the hope to which he has called you, what are the riches of his glorious inheritance in the saints,

Psalm 119:105 ESV

Your word is a lamp to my feet and a light to my path.

Psalm 119:105 ESV

Your word is a lamp to my feet and a light to my path.

Psalm 119:130 ESV

The unfolding of your words gives light; it imparts understanding to the simple.

Proverbs 1:7 ESV

The fear of the LORD is the beginning of knowledge; fools despise wisdom and instruction.

***

Our prayer is that God will plant in us hearts that recognize His goodness. We ask for hearts that will thank Him for all that we have. Our prayers could include gratitude for clean water, pure air, productive soil, healthy food, flourishing grass, fertile trees, beautiful mountains and plains, abundant rain, rest at night, productive days, the rising and setting of the sun, and the moon, loving homes, caring families, and compassionate friends. Above all, gratefulness for His goodness, mercy, and love, showering us with a life of peace and joy.

Bible Study Questions

Enlightenment

Are you the kind of woman (or man) who, when your feet hit the floor in the morning, the Devil says, "Oh, no, she (he) is up!"?

When you awake and give immediate thanks to God for the morning, the light, your life, and your strength – how does it make you feel?

When you sit down to breakfast, or any meal, do you give thanks to God for those who tilled the soil, planted the seeds, harvested, prepared, shipped, unloaded, placed on the grocery store shelf, checked you out at the register, bagged your purchases, and helped you carry them to the car? Do you understand all the steps that lead to the goodness of the abundance of food you eat?

Do you thank God for the joy of living?

PEACE AND CONTENTMENT

**"And let the peace of Christ
rule in your hearts,
to which indeed
you were called in one body.
And be thankful."**

**Colossians 3:15
Saint Paul**

Saint Paul (Saul), a devoted Jewish Leader, spurred on fellow members of the Jewish community to persecute Christians.

At that time, in that portion of the world, Christianity was considered a forbidden cult.   After Saul's conversion to Christianity, he began to build the church of God, one convert at a time.

During his many mission trips, he was shipwrecked multiple times, beaten, imprisoned, and suffered countless atrocities because of his beliefs.   Still, he continued onward in his missionary work of conversion of Jews and Gentiles to Christianity.

Paul, who had at one time denied that he was a follower of Jesus, tells us that in all things he found contentment. **"Not that I am speaking of being in need, for I have learned in whatever situation I am to be content. I know how to be brought low, and I know how to abound. In any and every** *circumstance, I have learned the secret of facing plenty and hunger, abundance, and need."* **Philippians 4:11-12**

***

Thoughts from Toni:

As Paul floated on a piece of wood in the Mediterranean Sea, hoping to make it to shore, he offered thanks to God for His peace.

Chained in a cold prison, perhaps to be slain by morning, he thanked God for being with him.

Fleeing a city in fear for his life, he thanked God for the path laid out before him.

Whether hungry or full, whether resting in a soft, warm bed or on a cold, stone floor, whether with friends or alone; he was content, satisfied, pleased with all things, and thankful for what he had, rather than longing for what he didn't have.

Paul, with his example of faith and trust in his Savior, established a goal that is worth our pursuing – contentment and a thankful heart.

***

What does God say about peace and contentment?

Hebrews 13:5 ESV

Keep your life free from love of money, and be content with what you have, for he has said, "I will never leave you nor forsake you."

Philippians 4:11 ESV

Not that I am speaking of being in need, for I have learned in whatever situation I am to be content.

Luke 12:15 ESV

And he said to them, "Take care, and be on your guard against all covetousness, for one's life does not consist in the abundance of his possessions."

1 Timothy 6:6-10 ESV
Now there is great gain in godliness with contentment, for we brought nothing into the world, and we cannot take anything out of the world. But if we have food and clothing, with these we will be content. But those who desire to be rich fall into temptation, into a snare, into many senseless and harmful desires that plunge people into ruin and destruction.

Proverbs 16:8 ESV

Better is a little with righteousness than great revenues with injustice.

Luke 3:14 ESV

Soldiers also asked him, "And we, what shall we do?" And he said to them, "Do not extort money from anyone by threats or by false accusation, and be content with your wages."

James 4:2 ESV

You desire and do not have, so you murder. You covet and cannot obtain, so you fight and quarrel. You do not have, because you do not ask.

Ecclesiastes 3:13 ESV

Also that everyone should eat and drink and take pleasure in all his toil—this is God's gift to man.

Ecclesiastes 3:12 ESV

I perceived that there is nothing better for them than to be joyful and to do good as long as they live;

Ecclesiastes 4:6 ESV

Better is a handful of quietness than two hands full of toil and a striving after wind.

***

Our prayer is that each person will fill their hearts with love for the Creator and the Son of God, Jesus Christ. We pray that the Holy Spirit, who is here to guide us, will fill our hearts with love and that we will have the knowledge that all we do is not for us but Him. With that knowledge, we will be content, our labors will be joyful, and our life filled with peace.

Bible Study Questions

Peace and Contentment

What did Paul mean when he said, "let the peace of Christ rule in your hearts?"

Paul could be intense in his messages. What do you believe he meant when he said that Christ, living in our hearts, is our call, in one body?

Are you thankful – every day – for the abundance of the life you have been given?

Living with a thankful heart makes everything better. Give thanks to God for all you enjoy.

Tomorrow
Fullness
Encouragement
Growth
Relationships
Perseverance
Enlightenment
Peace and Contentment

BIOGRAPHY   Toni Armstrong Sample

Toni retired from a successful career in Human Resource Management, Consulting, and years of presenting training and development programs across the United States. She moved from Erie, Pennsylvania to beautiful Greenwood, South Carolina, where she enjoyed painting, floral design, glass lampwork bead making, and dabbling in pottery.

Widowed for the second time in 2008, Toni turned her attention to writing. Previously published in magazines and journals, her writing has become a powerful and passionate way of expressing her faith in novels, novellas, autobiographical books, and devotionals. After almost twelve years of living alone, she has married a high school friend and now resides in Pickens, South Carolina, with her husband, Joe, and his Labradoodle, Kuma.

Toni has served tirelessly as an ordained elder, national speaker, retreat leader, Christian education leader, and women's group moderator. She contributed to the direction of the Erie, Pennsylvania American Red Cross, United Way, and the Erie School Board Advisory Committee, and several company boards. Toni was the leader of many workshops for the Manufacturer's Association of NW Pennsylvania and the National VA system. She is an active member of Rock Presbyterian Church.

Toni's lifetime of experiences helps her voice speak through her protagonists, who have substantial social and moral values coupled with spiritual strength housed in flawed human exteriors.

Other Books by Toni Armstrong Sample

<u>Out of Print and Revised Novels</u>
"Betrayal" Revision of "Distortion"
        "Distortion" (out of print)
"Creating Tomorrow" Revision of "Transparent Web of
                            Dreams"
        "Transparent Web and Dreams." (out of print)
"Zydeco and Oyster Pie" Revision of "The Glass Divider"
        "The Glass Divider" (out of print)
<u>Other novels:</u>
 "A Still Small Voice"
"Song of My Soul"
"Soup Kitchen Gala"
"When the Stars Fall"
"Other Plans"
"Fish Net Stockings"

<u>Autobiographical books:</u>
"A Buck Three Eighty"
"I Got Here as Fast as I Could"
"I'll Never Be the Same"

<u>Devotionals:</u>
"Wisdom is Sweet"
"Wisdom is Gentle"
"The Wisdom of Thankfulness"

Toni's inspirational stories are also available in many multi-author books.

www.ingramcontent.com/pod-product-compliance
Lightning Source LLC
Chambersburg PA
CBHW061720130726
47996CB00006B/2413